COWBOY PARK

WISCONSIN POETRY SERIES

Sean Bishop and Jesse Lee Kercheval, series editors
Ronald Wallace, founding series editor

COWBOY PARK

EDUARDO MARTÍNEZ-LEYVA

THE UNIVERSITY OF WISCONSIN PRESS

Publication of this book has been made possible, in part, through support from the Brittingham Trust.

The University of Wisconsin Press
728 State Street, Suite 443
Madison, Wisconsin 53706
uwpress.wisc.edu

Printed in the United States of America

Library of Congress Cataloging-in-Publication Data

Names: Martínez-Leyva, Eduardo, author.
Title: Cowboy Park / Eduardo Martínez-Leyva.
Other titles: Cowboy Park (Compilation) | Wisconsin poetry series.
Description: Madison, Wisconsin : University of Wisconsin Press, 2024. | Series: Wisconsin poetry series
Identifiers: LCCN 2024016358 | ISBN 9780299350840 (paperback)
Subjects: LCGFT: Poetry.
Classification: LCC PS3613.A78687 C69 2024 | DDC 811/.6—dc23/eng/20240426
LC record available at https://lccn.loc.gov/2024016358

Para Rebeca, Gloria y Lucie—
mis maestras de vida,
mis luceros, mi fortaleza y mi inspiración

I will no longer be made to feel ashamed of existing. I will have my voice…I will have my serpent's tongue.

—GLORIA ANZALDÚA

Border culture means . . . to smuggle dangerous poetry and utopian visions from one culture to another, desde allá, hasta acá . . . But it also means regresar y volver a partir: to return and depart once again, 'cause border culture is a Sisyphean experience and to arrive is just an illusion.

—GUILLERMO GÓMEZ-PEÑA

Contents

II

III

LEARNING THE LANGUAGE

To translate *confection*, my boy-tongue
nicked the hive's bloated colony.

No script or art to believe in, just sugar
paining the pink of me. I welcomed

polygamy, the plural of sting.
The strongest hurt came from the queen.

Her species (awe & expert)
was a light I asked to swig.

I was convinced she could give me
what I always wanted from a man.

COLORETE

For your seventh birthday, you asked for a shade
    of lipstick so dangerous your mother blessed herself.

It was the color of hell, no, of a tamer kind of Lucifer.
    The kind adorning the antagonist's lips on your screen,

painted gingerly on her puckered mouth. Sometimes
    pressed against an unmarked postcard, or smudging

the shirt collar of her nemesis's lover, or featured
    on the glossy pages of a magazine. You know the kind:

thick with a punch of perfume leaving you hurt
    or dazzled with a corked-up migraine for days.

You wanted to be mysterious, praised. Practiced
    raising a single eyebrow as you tested out the right tone

on your forearm. Stone-faced and regal. Imagined
    the tea parties and fancy invitations coming your way.

Mall-Kiosk-Red. Horror-Movie-Red. Bullet-Hole-Red.
    Posing-in-Front-of-the-Mirror-Red, the red of an all-night fire,

of an old suitcase leaving with your father. The red
    many say you're still too young for. Even after all these years.

Saint's-Execution-Red. Not the same red of shame shown across
    your family's face. No. Runaway-Red. Pickup-Truck-Red.

Liquor-Store-Robbery-Red. The red of thousands of vessels coursing
   through your body. A red bursting like the language of violence

you know so well. One-Night-Stand-Red. Hate-Crime-Red. A red staining
   the tips of your fingers. Panic-Button-Red. Star-Spangled-Banner-Red.

Conversion-Therapy-Red. The red that will one day suit your lips just right
   while getting yourself ready to leave this whole town in ashes.

ESL LESSON

*

To make sense of the world,
we stare at what's unrecognizable.

Unreachable. Before there is language,
we make sound, spell things inside our mouths,

expecting those objects to tumble out of us:
Paper clip. Pomegranate. Company.

We practice saying them over and over
until they lose all meaning, becoming stale.

Sometimes, the edges of those words are sharp
and final, smudging or staining us.

* *

Later, we learn to use our bodies as signals:
A thumb and pinky pressed against the side of our faces

becomes a telephone, curled fingers hold an invisible
cup we thirst over. A closed fist is a fist

and a fist can harm us. An index finger and thumb
become a handgun, and a gun will kill us.

* * *

To make sense of the world, we stare
at what's unrecognizable until it becomes familiar.

Too familiar. No longer strange to us.
We learn synonyms and antonyms; the definition for us:

Low-income. Brown. Faggots. From the other side of the tracks.

We learn fast. We learn how to run fast. We learn
how to outrun those things that will slaughter us.

THE BOY INSIDE THE GUN

There are fevers you still wish to forget,
the kind to singe off your eyebrows,
to keep you up with your brothers and the moon.

Sweat glimmering like a distant skyline on your skin.
Heat rising from your chest, thick as wolf's breath.
Even in sleep, you pose in a fanciful way,

in case you never wake up. The beginnings
of bruises already forming on your wrists and legs,
the only riches your father has ever given you.

Ribs poking out like the ribs of a sad accordion,
long abandoned by its owner. How criminal
to remember you this way. The youngest,

the hungriest bullet stuck inside
this old revolver. Rattling its tiny psalm
of grief. Shy-shaped one, sugar thief, hold on

to your questions as if they are your bones.
Whose voice will your throat house this time?
Whose heart are you driving yourself toward?

I NEVER WANTED TO SPEAK

of the house facing Cowboy Park
where my childhood pets are buried.

Eight small skulls scattered, each
a burned-out bulb keeping the fig tree

company, guarding the needles
I'd eventually unearth. My neighbor,

the infected queen, taught me
how to shoot down pigeons.

Think of them as compliments, he'd say.
By the time I was old enough to know

what he meant, it was too late
for him. Still, he slept inside me

for many seasons, cocking
his shotgun at a flinching sky.

Disguised in pill and sneer,
he waited for warmth to enter the body.

GRIEF WORKSHOP

Start with the bones
and work your way backwards,
go to the stillness
you once prayed about when young.
Go to the source of your earliest wounds.
The center of your darkness,
shaped somewhere inside you.
Even before you entered this world.
Molded inside God's fist.
Do you remember?
Or maybe start at a place
that's a little softer.
A family portrait. Each member
lined against a backdrop.
Shortest to tallest. The stoic poses
like those of generals having endured
the loss of a war. Now, fold one corner of it.
Who disappears? What is left of them?
Fold again until you can no longer see a face,
a lost brother, a cancer scare, a mass shooting.
Until it is thin, mean, careworn and creased.
Fold until it resembles a house, angular,
with jagged corners, made to look like the ones drawn
in your childhood. The stares of the ones
who hurt you the hardest live there.
Eyes only you could identify.
The boys who showed love with their knuckles.
The ones who lived looking up at the stars.

The ones we played with until it got dark. Fold it
like the lid to a coffin slowly lowered into the ground.
If there's enough room for a story,
there's room for sorrow and mercy. Forgiveness.
Imagine it. A mouth, the brightest, closing for good.

LONE STAR

Winter was never your season.
   Even in the desert you were cold.

Balled up your hands, stuffed them in your shirt.
   In the graveyard, you smoked

behind headstones, calling yourself
   the holiest one. Taking beatings

from your father to keep yourself warm,
   or so you said. When you were young,

your mom would sit you on her lap,
   hoping to sing away your shivers.

You were never interested in any of her stories
   unless there was a horse in them.

A single one, without reins or riders to bring him in.
   Savage. But you were one of the good guys.

Worked hard until you almost went blind
   and then worked some more. When fields froze over,

you'd think of the warmest touch:
   the vacant lots where it was just you and him.

Two shadows, two voices, all of that anger
   packed in. To make it out, you once told me,

you'd look at the sky, counting all the shooting stars,
   their infinite light, staring right back at you.

A boy, imagining the possibility of horses
   wildly running around heaven.

PORTRAIT OF MY MOTHER
IN HER YOUTH

She used to dance the twist and feared soldiers. Skipped school only once. Cut her hair short "like a boy." All her life. No beauty queens in her blood-line. No stares from older men. Just the way she liked it. Wore the same white dress and black orthopedic shoes. Posed with her hands on her lap as if holding an invisible book. Legs crossed at the ankles. She was a good shot; had a mean right hook. Hummed all of the English songs she knew to her only doll. Misunderstood the lyrics. Made eye contact with a run-away bull. On a dare, she hitchhiked to the outskirts of town. Rode a horse on her way back. Broke her arm riding a motorcycle. Appendicitis at age six. Chicken pox at age ten. In photographs, she's always left of center. She's had the same bad dream of being trapped in a strange cathedral; a colony of ants trailing up her leg. Her tongue, coated with the sticky words she's told to recite. There's no one to help her. Sadly. Give her the language she needs to make her way out.

SON OF A GUN

There's a boy in the room I'm renting
    who shows me his face
only in the dark. I can feel him.
He has a tongue, but doesn't speak.
    Wears his grief like a bad haircut,
    waiting for it to grow in or out.
    He could be a darling. The sweetest.
    Palpable. Part omen. Distracting.
    I talk to him sometimes.
    Tell him my secrets. He isn't one of them.
    I don't know what he believes in, what life
he's had before mine. I could swear
he looks like one of my brothers: Sunken-cheeked.
    Aching. Shivering. Lost. Every night,
    I bring him closer. Hold him before he disappears.
A single lantern intent on guiding me. The lone flame I cup,
    preserving its flickering light for as long as I can.

TORMENTA

The summer Angelo's wrists
were stitched up, we watched fishermen
struggle out of their wooden boats.

He told us, *Storms sound equally*
menacing in Spanish, but he could live
in that village, that language

of strong tongue, heat, and skin.
His rawboned body, a net draped across
the mud-black shore, where men piled

and piled their days' efforts.
In a less hurt age, he'd sift along
with us through that limp heap,

the delicate scales, so white
they were nearly transparent.
Back then we looked indifferent, faked

an accent, haggled a little for what
we could smuggle into the next world.

COMPOSITE SKETCH

A pause. She takes my face in her hands, tells the officer his nose is thinner than mine, *He looks just like this one*, she says, *only healthier, normal, not so dark*. The man's hands tremble as she explains this. The page between us is gray, nothing fancy. *Thinner still*, she continues, *a face you would love to marry*. I'm told to stay perfectly still, to lift my head a little more, a little more, into the light. Strong bones are difficult to reenact. And like that, my brother's face emerges, out of nothing, flared up and finessed by the hands that have spent years developing this craft, hour after hour putting together the noses, the eyes, the lips that have gone silent. The same indifferent hands that'll one day take him out of our world for good. But my mother, concerned the face is not pale enough, stresses how he had her skin: delicate, stubborn. But it's late, too late. With a single loud clap, the officer brushes off whatever's left of my brother, a small cloud of ash rising from his hands before settling into the dust.

I WAS ONLY A BOY

A pair of descending stars
   could persuade me to do
unthinkable things. Find me
   hotboxing in cars, parked deep in the desert.
Then sleeping next to
   a man, eyelid-heavy, his skin
the kind some would kill for: white
   and more experienced than mine.
I wasn't a savage then, but to him I was
   the seedy back alley where he could
lose himself and all of his belongings.
   He liked it that way. The danger
my body posed for him. Even before
   that body became dangerous to me.
Carrying fake IDs and shoplifted
   cologne, I was incorrigible. Harbored
many selves which had dead-end lives.
   I plotted a perfect ending for each one:
tracing their nonlinear route as if tracking
   a lost package. Every step I took was reckless,
but coldly calculated. All with the intention of disappearing
   up the stairs, never coming back down.
Only I didn't have a two-story house, let alone
   a single room to run to. Had no home.
Nothing was sitcom-pretty. No very special episode.
   No laugh track. I became a face
inside a face inside another face. Mild-mannered and poorly lit.
   Tasted blood inside a roach-smeared rest stop,

where a figure loomed over me, looking for his void to fill.
   Boy to fill. You get the idea. He slipped his thumbs inside
my mouth, called me his sickly-sweet stereotype,
   asked me to pout before telling me
to keep my eyes fixed on his as if he were the night sky,
   or two gracious lights leading me to heaven.

PORTRAIT OF AGING FATHER

Loose teeth. A small bout of depression.
I can't imagine your heart as anything but a fist.
No one to hold you back. You drank.
The neighborhood. The city.
Even the perfume bottles.
Father of insulin and bad words.
Dipping dead scorpions in bleach, you then set them
ablaze to prevent infestation. Saved the stingers.
What else did you keep? Father of failed
child support payments. Born into the business
of suffering you said. Not blond. Superstitious.
One glass eye. When you call, you do it anonymously.
Father of syringe and black coffee. You once
tried to remove your tonsils with rusted pliers.
The only gun you held was aimed at your head.
Father of fits and minimum wage.
Once, you begged for my tongue to dream
in another language. Soon you will be a ghost
without enough to haunt. I help button your coats
and shirtsleeves, buckle your seat belt.
I place your hand on the inside of my elbow
when guiding you through places you deem
too dark. Now, I'm just a blurred blemish
you can barely see.

WITH JESUS IN OUR MOUTHS

The God we knew spoke only Spanish.
Didn't have the face

of an old bottle cap, crushed
and buried in dirt like us.

Mom would go to bed con el Jesús en la boca.
Embers rising from her lips.

In a black-and-white film, the child actor
discovers Him in the attic of a monastery.

Abandoned. Feeds Him bread and wine.
Takes off His crown of thorns.

By morning, no one believes him.
Then, one day, God removes the boy's name,

tells him to close his eyes
before taking him for good.

We prayed to be like that child,
covered in light and scooped up

by something tender, glorious. Held gently
for once in our lives.

PORTRAIT OF MY MOTHER STUDYING FOR HER CITIZENSHIP EXAM

She sits on the corner of her bed, head tilted to one side. Licks the tip of her thumb and flips through the thick booklet, trying to remember where we left off. Two weeks ago, the mint-colored Bronco parked in the neighbor's driveway. The youngest one left in handcuffs and they haven't heard from her since. My mother sighs, "Pobre de México, tan lejos de Dios y tan cerca de los Estados Unidos." I am ten. And so far away from God, I feel. Angelo and I take turns teaching her, tracking English like dirt into our home. The only savior they tell us we need. If only it could be that simple and true. To build her a life out of mud and syllables, of saliva, colonies, and state capitals, treaties and phrases coined during a long-ago war, written in a textbook-pretty cursive. *Give me liberty or give me death*, she repeats. Even the birds' names she has to learn. And after all those evenings, rehearsing and memorizing the mythology of it, no one could prepare her for the early morning raid, the strip searches at the border, the child who gets deported. If you ask me, it's hard to believe in God, especially when years later she's still forced to dodge slurs and bullets from a white man who aims a gun at her in the supermarket. *Give me liberty or give me death*. But for now, she'll settle at the corner of her bed, skimming through lines and sentences, narrowing her eyes as her fingers move to the following page, mouthing out words, unfolding a wrinkled map she smooths open with her hands, pausing before using her index finger to trace the dotted lines. She pores over these texts for hours and hours. Focused. Determined. Always pensive and gentle. Careful but intentional, like when combing for ticks on the head of her firstborn son.

ANGELO

Noun   My noun   My verb too   A box of rusty adjectives
Body of light   Seemingly lost to history
Patron Saint of Bronzer and Bragging Rights
Three-chord heart waiting to be strummed
The handsomest ballad in Texas
Socks pulled up to the knees
Mi ingles   My Spanish   My foreign town
A carbon copy for grief   Mom's assembly line
of disappointments   A synonym for trauma
A dirty white tank top   A collapsable shadow
The fifteen-minute segment on the six o'clock news
How to use *you* in a sentence

He was last seen wearing: a denim shirt, cigarette-tight pants.
Gold chain and Stetson hat. Snake-skin boots.
Unarmed. Black hair. Brown eyes. 5'5.
Pronounced ANG-jeh-lo. Sin papeles.
Health status: Unremarkable. No visible scars.

People think your name is classic
formal   wholesome   refined
You're the expired prescription at the bottom of a purse
The mound of ground I'm meant to archive
Open it up like every door in the house   *Leave it open*
my therapist says   Not shrine-worthy
An incision   A lacunae   My pet caesura

Eventually, everything will become a ghost to someone.

SIN DOCUMENTOS

Of God, we only understood His wrath, and still, we spoke about Him
as if He were an older brother. Another one of us: brown and buzzed cut,

running into the ditch, learning about the dangers of tall grasses.
Of bullets. Uninsured. On weekends, He'd drive across the bridge

to get drunk off two-dollar liquor. Listened to country music
while sucking bone marrow when afternoons got cold and lonely.

Not the good kind of songs. The ones with heft and heartache,
pulled from the deepest wells of His throat. Untranslatable.

Then, like the rest of us, He'd return. Remorseful. Heavy-breathed
and bloodshot, speaking another language. Smelling like a burnt museum

with souvenirs He'd smuggled inside His pockets: A silver tooth.
A stuffed bird. A dried-up seahorse. A miracle. A new wound for us to share.

DON'T LOOK BACK, LITTLE HALO

The officer misspells your brother's name,
and you correct him, *It's like Angel but with an o.*
He doesn't listen. Mom doesn't care.
And before repeating yourself, she squeezes
your arm. Whispers, "No digas nada, así pensaran que es gringo."
You understand. They'll look for him faster that way,
if they think he's white. American.
You're used to this type of amputation,
of mistranslation, having been a contortionist most of your life.
Tear up your name to make it easier on yourself.
It isn't shame, but maybe a smudge of it
lingers. Think of those times you flicked away
accents and diphthongs on certificates and birthday cakes.
Or when a man turned down a second date
because he couldn't say your name correctly,
or the friend who asks for your advice on naming
her unborn son, something palatable, so that if he ever goes
missing, like your brother, he can come back to her
unscathed. Complete. Whole as the halo
you are told to truncate. Whole as the circle or letter
at the end of Angelo's name. As the shape
of a mother's mouth howling in laughter or distress.

STILL LIFE WITH POST-TRAUMATIC STRESS DISORDER

My mother sits
in the eggshell-colored

waiting room, listening
to the clock's tinny rhythm,

the worst kind of
purgatory.

Spread like tarot
across the table

are dog-eared magazines
and brochures, written

in a language
she doesn't understand.

Sharp headlines, boldly
staring back at her.

She doesn't dream
anymore, is a citizen

of a country where
the dialect is seeped

in anger. Deep-rooted.
A country that trusts

in God but not in her.
There is a map burning

violently inside.
River muck extracted

from her lungs.
An invisible bullet

traces a path
around her body.
                *
Politicians say she's one
of the luckier ones.

Send gift baskets.
Pardon her debt.

Doctors say
it will take months—

years—before
she can open the curtains again,

watch the news, slice
a pomegranate,

and not think about a heart
slowly beating until it stops.

No one ever prepares you for it,
she says. *The way a face looks*

when life is fleeting from it.
In the meantime, they tell us

to keep her away
from any and all violence.

Distract her with pills
and soothing songs.

                *

"Canta y no llores."
Studies tell us trauma,

like grief, is nonlinear.
Expect flashbacks. The first night

will be the most difficult.
"Porque cantando . . . se alegran

los corazones." Officials say
she doesn't have the right paperwork.

Want to confirm that we are legal.
Related. Documentation

goes back and forth, floating
like sailboats, timidly reaching land

in dark hours. A police officer
informs us that several Americans

will experience a mass shooting
at some point in their lives.

Better to get it out of the way.
The officer wants me to translate,

explain it to her. *Ya no quiero recordar.*
She'd rather go home. Marked

by a haunting scar, she wishes to sleep
through the noise pollution.

Away from the din, the phone calls,
the fire alarms, the sirens and shrills,

hammering through her
like that ancient doctrine nailed

to a sacred door all those years ago,
written and rewritten, transformed,

from mouth to mouth, into a language
she still has a hard time understanding.

PORTRAIT OF ANGELO
WITH HIS POSSESSIONS

The scene: a dead crow, a slingshot, and a winking boy, figures
preserved inside a 4×5, 5×7 inch photograph. The boy

doesn't know any better, but stands with the confidence
of an outlaw towering over his prey. Shirtless. Hemlock

shrouding his shoulders. Jeans tucked inside his boots.
On his left side, a toy holster. What does he hide behind his back?

It's too hard to tell. Life hasn't gotten a hold of him yet.
Before the graveyard shifts and beer runs, the fistful

of uppers and drive-bys, before the handcuffs, he was a boy,
thin-wristed, naive, harmless. One day, mischief will lead him

through a sliding door, cutting him down to the nerve,
where innocence once pulsed. But behind this picture frame,

he's still young. He'll stay with me a little while longer:
suspended at the edge of this memory, this rare moment.

Proud of his small victory. With his one eye always locked
on me. A reminder that only one of us will make it back home.

CONFIRMATION

That year we grew more and more
into our shared grief, hid in the ditch,
marred by snow mold,

to drink bum wine,
then gossip about stars, mothers,
you-know-what. We rubbed beeswax

in our hair, watched our ends split.
On Sundays, we'd stare at the back
of the schoolteacher's glowing head.

Sweat halo, no bigger than a mare's
bite. After the lake thawed, and his body
surfaced, I heard his lips

were slightly open, as if in a calm,
permanent prayer. You heard this too.

ALMOST-GRIEF

Days after the shooting, none of us spoke,
but we could feel the hard shape of harm making a nest

inside each one of us. *It's almost grief, adjacent to it,*
the therapist said. A bullet-sized bird, rupturing us.

We became fragments of a small town,
one we would typically drive through:

Twenty-four-hour diners, split-level homes,
a condemned water tower, skating rinks,

and abandoned warehouses as far as the eye could see.
Neighborhoods that once whirled by until they were just a blur.

Nothing noteworthy, we thought. But they meant something
to someone. Everything. At one point or another.

Little town of magnificence. We didn't know it then.

II

SCENES FROM THE
BONE ORCHARD

*

The first man my mother loved was a cowboy.
Boot-heavy, dark cloud of a man. Hardly holy.
Drank everything neat. He wasn't neat, carried
his headstone wherever he went.

For years, he was an apparition.
A candle dimly fading on her nightstand.

* *

My mother kissed the feet of the second man she loved.
Wooden arms stretched wide on the cross.
Traced His open wounds with her index finger.
She rubbed her lipstick smudge off his feet.

Something was always determined to leave a mark.

* * *

The Angelos I've known spent half of their lives
near Cowboy Park, surviving on discount deli meats
and dark liquor. I've known several of them: some who fed me,

some who left me for dead. Sad, mean ones.
Some who disappeared, others who got locked away
in dreams: the doors of their world—deadbolted.

Some who were obsessed with drowning, who lived
in broken-down cars near cemeteries.
Who lived through a midlife crisis.

Ones who made it into a first draft, who stood curbside,
warming their hands with their breath. Those whose hair
went white. Who never taught me to believe in something

that wasn't cold, sharp, or dirty. Hardworking ones,
whose pupils are as dark as a sleepless night. And those
who catcalled and barked around the streets,

tugging on the sleeves of my vulnerability.
Pants down, dicks out. Angelos picking away
at their addictions as if peeling an apple apart,

removing the skin bit by bit, before someone's hunger
could plunge into its sparkling core: the source of light
and shame. In Spanish, the act of coring an apple
is called "descorazonar," to dishearten.
All these years, I've kept my hands away
from everyone's heart, including my own.

I'd always love the things that bruised so easily.

PORTRAIT OF A BOY ON THE OTHER SIDE OF A GLORY HOLE

Most wounds are circles, so it's no surprise
you'll find me here. Alone. On my knees, on evenings
when the moon hangs low. The brown boy
behind the hole—not quite the size
of a cave or a cigarette burn. Splitting open
my lips the way a saint parts his mouth to banish thirst
or famine or to corral his flock. I have stories
and sadness to share, have known men
who moan like injured dogs, others like horses
off to the glue factory. Their dignified shape
reduced by the deep vermilion of my rim.
I used to be scared. Eyes locked on the ceiling.
My trembling voice wrapped around their hard-ons.
They only feel me through the hollow they occupy,
briefly. I am all mouth. Cavities and throat.
Obedient. Never see, never touch.
Some call for Jesus as if that were my name.
I have lost so much around here.

SMALL VICES

Snow illuminated the park
   and you wanted to die. That winter

you slept with a saucer of water
   under your bed. Every night. Woke up to find nothing

but the off-white stare of the empty cup.
   Spelled out your fantasies on my upturned

palms. They were dirty. Unsayable.
   Between us ran a long line of insomniacs

and addicts. Bad habits. Missing history
   we wanted to piece back together. Stitch it

like an heirloom displayed behind a glass vitrine.
   We looked for signs in cards and tea.

In the language our muscles made at night.
   The nearness of stars, in songs.

As the storm hit, reaching past our hips,
   you read Russian novels to feel less morose.

Said you loved the word "morose" more than me.
   Locked yourself behind your grin-wrinkled face

which you believed looked like a foreign town
    pillaged years ago. Curtainless. Flags at half-staff.

When the lights finally went out, you tried your hardest
    covering all of this up with your hands.

My voice was the only thing keeping us warm.

COWBOY PARK

Take me to where the river is thin but unforgiving.
I've saved my pennies, kept a man in my room
who said he smelled you all over the sheets.
I had a hard time believing him.
Take me to where diamondbacks hiss
when they're about to strike or fuck.
Take me stupid and broke, hungover
on weekends, looking for a place to crash.
Take me to where the only fox I've ever seen was dead.
Take me mercilessly: skinned knees and jacked-up teeth,
a decade's worth of thirst. Lay your good hands on me
the way only a saved man can. Go on. Save me.
Rough up my hair a bit. Show me your heart, cowboy.
What else do I have to wait for, huh?
You-beautiful-guilt-free-creature.
I wish you'd say this and mean it.

VAQUERO

You want to put your darkness in me. All of it.
As if it always belonged to me. Ruthless

rattlesnake of a man. Riding shotgun down
the highway, not ashamed. What could possibly

possess you? To think an entire night could fit
in me. Slip inside the black sky's haunches and limbs.

The patient stars with their glittery thighs.
The forearms. Deep in the heart of Texas.

I could ruin you. Spend an afternoon with my head
on your chest. The wild-wild-west of you sleeping

off an all-night bender. I could. Get used to this.
Bent over on the side of the road, taking in the violet

knuckles and wrists of the evening. *I've had my share
of roughnecks*, I confessed one day, while watching

a woman dancing with a python wrapped around her
shoulders at the local fair. *I wasn't impressed.*

One of your favorite scenes features two men
stuffing another one with their erections

and any thick facsimiles. They take turns.
Eiffel Tower. Double penetrating, before punching him

on the back of the head until unconscious. Looks
peaceful when it's done. You made me watch over

and over, refusing to touch me unless I got it right.
Let's try it tonight, you said. I've never been to France,

but in Spain, folks call their denim jeans—vaqueros.
As in, *I'm going to slip into my vaqueros. Take my vaqueros*

to the bar. Hang my vaqueros on the clothesline
once they're clean. I like the way my vaqueros feel

when they're on me. Nothing gets between me
and my vaqueros. The only cowboy I know

offers to buy my brothers a round of beer
when they want to square up with him. The cowboy

I know is just like my brothers. Coils his hot-dumb
breath around my neck. Threatens to smash a bottle

across my face. Tightens his body when he sees me
seize up. Around here, we love hard, drink even harder.

Back in the day, ranchers burned the animals that died
instead of burying them. The way their fathers taught

them to do so. Watched until nothing was left but a carcass
steaming like winter breath. No man passed down

this knowledge to me. I have no one to pass down this knowledge to.
If every cowboy has a sad song, I'm afraid you are mine

to perform. I know you by heart and bloodstains. Hold you
in my mouth until you become my third language, seared

and branded. Nothing pretty to see. Every now and then, I enjoy
the weight of your body thrashing against mine, while thinking

of all the animals going up in flames. How nobody mourns anymore.
Not like they used to. You once told me about a recurring dream,

where a girl swallows a snake that grows and grows inside her stomach
like a seed wanting to live, be something special, admired.

Whose gut do I need to grow in again? I tell you if I had to, I could easily
swallow a snake without feeling any remorse. We both know that's a lie.

SHOW PONY

I'm your trick, one and only,
your dirty boy. Prop me
against the wall.
Just how you like it.
Young and still kind.
Desperate for milk. Feed me
from your cupped hand,
the same hand you'll slap me
with later. *You can't know love
unless you learn pain first*, you
say. I don't understand.
How to submit, be broken in.
Be good. *Good, good boy.*
I mistake the word *discipline*
for *disciple. Same shit.* You tell me.

AND GOD PUNISHED HIM
FOR BEING DISOBEDIENT

Someone named you after a flood.
As though you were doomed
from the beginning. An overturned boat
uncovered during low tide,
at the edge of the Atlantic.
Slowly splintering, stripped
to the whitest bark on the tree of your origin.
You wondered about the ways
you kept hurting yourself.
How everything starts with beauty
and ends in violence. A wreckage
no one remembers. The men
didn't know where to place their sin.
You lay next to the ocean, letting the salt
harden your blood, your skin.
As if all of this could slake your thirst. Cleanse you.
   As a child, your mother rocked you in her arms
   sang to you about a boy befriending
   a fish, coaxing it out of the water to play.
   He was lonely—the fish—gullible.
   Didn't know any better.
   Never forget, she whispered.
   A young mouth can be the cruelest,
   has the sharpest hunger.
   Even God's son was naive enough
   to trust a group of men.
   They'll betray you someday
   she said, *if you don't listen.*
   Believe me. They'll take you by the hands,
   if not by your lips.

GOD MAY SQUEEZE BUT WON'T STRANGLE YOU

Forgive me for thinking I was always right.
His hands were benign and impressive.
Good enough for the heavens.
If I gave him my neck, would he take it?
Here, sprawled in the hour of honeyed light,
dying grass, and possibility. Then I remember,
A few miles down the road,
someone was slipping a hand down
A tight pair of swim trunks.
When a boy got called a pussy,
Face shoved in the cold, wet ground. Waves lapping
blood and sand from his face. "Dios aprieta pero no ahorca."
If this is true, I should feel reassured
in the blessings of my own skin and where they take me.
It's all about perception, I tell myself, peeling off my clothes,
Pretending to be someone else. Knees buckling,
mouth agape in exclamation. *Oh, Lord!* I say. As I surrender.

TORERO

What is it about the spring that brings
the bull out of me? That purpled tongue

sticking out of my pouting lips,
the better to bruise you with, my dear.

There is so much rage inside this dark body.
So much joy you want to stab into me

when you're shrouded in your suit of stars.
Tonight there are no witnesses, no crowd to pelt

you with petals. No *boleros* left to sing.
Only the sharp, triumphant danger that thrusts you

to the tipped-over beast, waiting to be torn.

MUD SONG

You know it when you hear it.
   The swag in a man's voice
tempting, lulling you. Drunk
like a whistling locomotive.
   What it brings. What it takes.
Show me what you've seen.
   Young, callous body. Smeared
with hard work and some kind of strife.
   The pills in the medicine cabinet.
The missing factory girls. Young boys in chokeholds.
They left home too. Someone loved them.
   Waited all night for their return.
(Still waiting.) Wrote them letters in their fanciest penmanship.
They were the heavy-studded sky sparkling in family albums.
   No more floods or hurricanes, but a different
type of catastrophe for mothers to cradle.
   The old southern way of life: White Pontiacs.
   Moonshine. Fringe and rhinestones.
Bible-black pomade. A smelter town without a lovers' lane.
   The right kind of debauchery leaning against
your conscience. Here comes your brother,
   after a round of bloody knuckles, Smear the Queer.
Snorting lines from a tabletop. Mercy.
   How much are you willing to listen? Overlook?
      As a kid, you ran with the rest of them, shirtless
   behind the school, looking to throw your body around.
      You ran for miles until the noise became music.

Danceable. Inescapable. Thumping through your veins.
    Gospel. Some days, you'll catch yourself
humming to it. Assuaging the high-pitch cruelty
    you once held in your lungs.
Some days, you'll lift your hands in praise,
    like a good little boy.

ESTRELLITA

He punched me until all I saw were tiny, flickering stars.
Miniature cowboys riding on silver horses.
He loved me. I thought. He loved me
when he gripped my neck, when he spat Valium
down my throat. He loved me
until I was out like a bulb. My dreams becoming red and black,
blotches. I couldn't see past the blemishes. I was filthy.
Terrified. A muddy puddle at the end of a crosswalk,
hard to avoid. Back then, everyone wanted to be famous.
Ended up at parties I was never invited to.
In simpler times, this could have been romantic.
An embrace. Arms wrapped around my neck.
He approached me from behind.
With his right hand, he covered my eyes.
How many chapters does this book have?
He wanted to skip to the less graphic parts.
Looked away, but cared enough to wince.
He knocked me from here until all I could see
were galaxies. Ones I didn't know existed.
Too many to name. I didn't want to stay here long.
I was cold. Secretly, I wanted to be colder.
But I became the light that drags itself across the dark sky.
Igniting the spaces of a ransacked room,
his work clothes tossed over the dining room chair.
I unfolded myself, an outstretched hand. Empty.
I learned to keep going.
Despite all of this or because of it.

GOD MADE DIRT, AND
DIRT DON'T HURT

They say the only language God understands is thirst.
Listens to that craving rumbling out of your mouth
more than any sweet or piercing prayer. And that the ground,
and anything slamming against it doesn't belong to Him.
Truth be told, I grew up believing that nothing precious
came from dirt, was careful not to spill food, a drink, trip,
tumble or fall. Never sat on grassy hills or sand at the beach,
never picked anything up, making sure I was absolved.
So that no one could mockingly say, "Te chupó el diablo!"
But, when a blue-eyed man, using his breath as bait, led me
by my wrists down the corridors of his thirst, I complied.
Was God listening then? I wanted to heed (hand to the heavens,
I did). I believed him when he said I was precious
while making me lap up sand to make mud with my spit.

TEASE

You like me when I'm small. Trembling. Take my chin in your hand. Rub me between your fingers. A piece of fabric. You like me. Quiet. Coated in ash. Riddled with bullets. Something you could sink your teeth into. Count the injuries. The abrasions. Come feel the wounds. Give me your hands. You've taken the pulse from mine. Put your arms around me. You know you want to. I'm your little machine. Your history of traumas. Rough spot. Rough house. Museum of heat. Donkey Moon. Souvenir. Comb the desert shrub for a piece of me. This is my love language. So talk dirty to me. Call me your mule. Señorita Tacón. Your Tumbleweed. I can be prickly. If you want me to. The cut on the roof of your mouth. Half-bitten morsel. Grip me like handlebars. Grip me like your life depended on it. It's true. Everything you've heard about me—true. I wouldn't lie. I shine. The way blood shines as it's leaving the body.

ADULTERY

To feel a little less dirty,
I wipe my hands on my shirt
while thinking of someone else's guilt.

Those men with doll eyes
who tugged at the edges of my appetite
lapping filth after filth from me—

I never asked for this. A world ago,
I wore all white, knelt until my knees bled,
collected shiny objects beneath the bed

to illuminate what gutted me.
In sleep, I still flail my arms, reaching
for a tongue to warm my mouth.

Bring movement back to my lips.
I was gentle with my words, spoke
the way my master spoke. Tossed myself

around in a stranger's wet dream
and remained nothing but a blue silhouette;
collapsible as a night closing in on itself.

Each dawn, I wake with lesions all over me.
No one dares to question or explain.

GOD GAVE YOU HANDS,
SO USE THEM

Mother, tonight the devil's on my tongue and he's not letting go.
And he doesn't look like my father, but maybe a little to you

when the light hits at a certain angle. You asked me to believe in God,
knowing that to do so means I must believe in darkness too.

I think of those times when you talked your way out of situations
with your fists. Knocking teeth out, then later knocking some sense

into me. How could I compete? How could I not do the same?
You prayed I was born a boy to avoid the pain this world ripped into you.

But I am severed in other ways. Your skirt's hem, still unspooling, slowly.
Raised by your belt buckle, broom, and grit. I wanted to be enough.

Mother of light, I am your darkness, where strangers come and unzip me
to reveal, then revel in, the traumas I tried to name and bury.

When young, you told me to offer this up to the Lord, surrender
the way I surrender to vices too shameful to disclose. I obeyed.

Had the neighborhood on its knees at the sight of me.
Listen, I never meant for the men to sing, to sin.

HORSESHOE

Men want to make you into rust.

Men want to put things inside you.

You're not a jewel or a music box,

not worth a pinch or ballad.

Back-roads stew. Less than a tickle.

They stick their fingers down your throat.

Call you: Blue meat. Spittoon. Horseshoe.

Zoquete. Store-brand bread. Blow you like dust.

Third world. Little Flower Church. Eight-story

brick building with no fire escape. Pay dirt.

Artificial-American accent. Vete por lo oscurito.

They want you to wear a red dress

while carrying a rose between your teeth. Backless.

Low-plunging neckline. Wear you like a lucky rabbit's paw.

Turn you around, upside-down question mark.

Breed you. Ride you until the box spring sings. Stings.

Ride you like a mechanical bull. Ride you

till the cows come home. Ride you till you never come

home, till you're nothing but a *MISSING* poster.

Tied to a post. Faded letters. Creased documents

over a coroner's desk. Stacks on stacks. Coffee stained.

Till they conjugate you in the past tense. *You asked for it.*

Newspaper clippings underneath a mattress.

Colorín colorado este cuento se ha acabado.

The frayed ends of a ribbon, yellowing.

The stuffed fawn mounted on the wall.

The wooden crucifix nailed at the end of your hallway.

The one you no longer visit or worship.

NOW YOU'RE TALKING

right into my ear, screaming, actually,
an insult crawling down the littlest muscle
before striking the spine. I don't see blood,
but I can feel it: rising, hard.
Stranger, don't you know my mind
is more than a nest of candy or a sugar
cube dissolving with one good lick?
I'm a different kind of tough,
the queen with too much
powder up her nose, spending nights
in a sweat, serving lust, spinning
a fan of feathers into light.
Too pretty to give a shit.
In another life, you could've had me
without a hand over your mouth,
a knife trembling around your neck.
I've known your kind of thirst,
sheepish to the core, suckling the life
out of your face. I'll keep a handsome
secret for years and years. Let me lean
closer to your filth. Tonight, we'll see
whose arrow is the first to touch the sky.

ODE TO A LEATHER HARNESS

Whatever daddy wants, daddy gets.
Swarmed in the nightclub candor.
You are expensive, the king of red lights.
Fastened around the waist and neck, stretched
to pull shoulders back like the firm grasp
of a lover. Up and ready. Rubbed raw
in all the right ways. Will you be my throne?
The darkest jewel in my crown?
I could wear you every day to remember
the feeling of pleasure, of being alive.
Cage me inside someone else's fantasy
or punishment. Make me dig
for pearls in the Atlantic with my teeth.
My studded-eyelet albatross, show no mercy.
What do you hold up or in? All of my secrets
are tall and unforgivable. In your strange arms
is where I cave. Unravel the way
a holy shroud unravels at a first touch.
I want you like I want a tighter grip.
My kink of kinks. My Old and New Testament.
Come closer. I imagine you and I spinning
on the misty dance floor, liquor-stained
and covered in glitter until last call.
I keep all of my fetishes near my chest
is what I tell those who want to be
my walk-of-shame, see me on all fours.
Don't worry, you can't hurt
what's already hurting. My double-dog dare you.
My shameless, luminous one. It's you I turn to.
Glinting like the sharpest knife in the drawer,

like the only thing that matters
at this juncture. *My one and only master.*
I see no harm in this one-sided embrace.
You are mine. Together we are
a horse-drawn carriage, our very own heaven,
and no prayer stuck in my throat
will make me any sweeter.

BRACERO WITH A TATTOO OF THE VIRGIN MOTHER

Once, you were like me: impulsive,
a little rebellious, dark. Dumb enough
to let a man mark you on your forearm.
Said it wouldn't last forever, said it wouldn't hurt.
That wasn't the first time you were lied to.
The first time you felt pain. You wish you could
undo it, the way one untangles hair
knotted by wind and dirt. The same way
one might reverse a spell. Patiently.
You used to believe all spirits were blue.
Said they'd visit at night and tug on your bare feet
before stumbling out of the room.
There was no devil yet, only walls of smoke,
plenty of wars, and owls which you avoided—
their blond stares were the most dangerous portents
you knew. You were the tattooed tragedy of your kin.
Dreamed of horses galloping past your home.
Most afternoons, you'd take a single razor blade
to your skin, gently brushing its sharpness
against your upturned arm, rubbing and rubbing
until the inked face no longer resembled the face
of a mother mourning her crucified son.
You wanted to make it to heaven. But you were still branded,
a smudge, an apparition some might call a miracle.
    Once, I was like you: bringing tears to the only woman
who cared for me. I can't remember the first time I broke her,

but her image remains branded inside. She is the innermost wound,
her cry spreads itself outward, rippling my blood.
She won't let me sleep. What drums up from me is her passion,
her grief, a wake of mothers praying, echoing like the hard-steady
sounds of the wild horse you never rode, named, or owned.

NEGATION LITANY
FOR A FALLEN GOD

No more drunk dancing at the Bronco Inn.

No more brush fires, late-night cruising.

No more memorizing license plate numbers,

doing math with a concussion. No more missing days.

No more burner phones, screwdrivers,

Russian Red lipsticks, and dirty blonde wigs.

No more *who-would-you-like-me-to-be?*

No more *you-have-me-confused-for-someone-else.*

No más tragos coquetos.

No more entertaining tragic hands, poppers,

underage fantasies, milk fetishes.

No more ungloved nights.

No more falling for the ones who'd spit and gloat.

No more dry heaving in Flea Grove.

No more back-alley root canals.

No more *face down, ass up, that's the way we like to . . .*

No more lapping up Ácido del Diablo from tattooed palms.

No more harvesting silence.

No more need for prayers like this one.

No more swallowing blood and coughing up trenzas.

THERE IS LITTLE LEFT TO SAY ABOUT HARM

I rode until the Lord said stop.
   The horses drowned themselves
that summer. They'd prefer that over the heat or thirst
rippling through the town. So hot you could see it,
so hot you swore the devil was ironing his clothes.
   At night, I slept with sweets in my mouth
to lure all the missing ones back from who-knows-where.
   I had heart then. Pity. Stared a little too long
at the men who'd proselytize on weekends.
The whites of their starched shirts, sharp and bright
like the life outside of this one. I asked to be good.
No hard hand, no god or cowboy could dissuade me.
   What I looked for was not strap or stirrup,
   grit or bit, but the temptation in the flounce of ruffles,
gingham. The dangers of a swishy walk. The soft gloves hiding
freckles and bad intentions. The heaviest, elegant fabrics
couldn't help me either. Others tried to mark me,
make me like the rest. Pin me to the ground.
Face down. A firm grip around my neck.
   A knee pushing against my back.
I dressed like a star, discovering my brilliance, my losses.
   What it takes to survive.

NOSTALGIA CRUISING

Under a canopy of red lights, the locals gather to watch an aging porn star climax on TV—tanned skin slick with sweat and oil. No storylines or props, just him, muted, spread over a burgundy bed. He is good. Toned. All blood and muscle and veins and salt. Necks crane towards the screen to get a better look. From downstairs, music pumps into the edges of the club, which a patron informs me used to be "the spot." Someone sings off-key about feeling homesick. In the bathroom, a man of about my age, or younger, collects himself before his first score of the evening. Takes deep breaths of something powder-blue. Stares at me from across his dim corner. I can't tell whether it's a look of pity or that of a mad dog. It's October, and the sea air brings a bitter, slow, quivering to this hour. The last days before each shop, one by one, boards up for the season. I came here to see where the masters have worked, drank, danced, worshipped, and surrendered to temples of flesh. To the divine, the blacked out, the lost ones finding their way home. Spilling into the streets, where their passion slinks back into the body's grip. Those beaming constellations, points of reference. I come to honor them. Bathe in their light. Some are angry. Some sad. Some grateful. On the screen, the star's face relaxes, pleased with his completion. He has blessed us. And everyone claps before it all goes black, then loops back up again. And again we see the same face; the camera steadies on him as he disrobes, flexes, and sucks in his breath as if to say, *if there's an afterlife, please, let this be it.*

III

WHEN I SPOKE THE
LANGUAGE OF DONKEYS

Sit still, you told me. Give the desert
    what belongs to the desert. A vessel of dust
is all you will be, dimwit. Be a dear and shape up,

brown boys get sad too, you know.
    There is no need for others to see. Cuídate.
To them, you are an entire village stuffed inside

an envelope. When they do see you:
    body made criminal, body, lust factory.
Body, the thing dogs chase after.

You were born at night and that is why
    you are so dark. Leave it alone.
Straighten your voice.

Can you name this bird?
    Can you quote Shakespeare?
Are you fluent in donkey? Do you aim

to disappoint? You are the goddamn zoo
    and all the animals in it.
Keep your hands visible,

they are as small as sparrows' nests,
    but still a threat to others. Never carry flowers
unless you are heading to a funeral.

Hold your head as straight as your voice.
   Let me tell you, the door you came
from was always cracked. Can't you see?

Count the days but you won't hear back.

AFTER THE SHOOTING, YOU HAVE A PANIC ATTACK IN THE SUPERMARKET

On a Saturday morning, you drive across Francis Scott Key Bridge, mindful of cyclists and joggers; the tourists blocking the sun from their eyes to catch a glimpse of the imperious monument looming over everyone. Another stone god they've come to worship. But you're here because you're hungry. Stuff your cart with spreads and fancy cheeses that, in another life, you could never afford, walk through the shiny, polished aisles, greeting others with a nod or short, quick smirk. You feel warmth around your eyes. Open the carton of eggs to examine each one. Looking for cracks, checking the expiration dates. When all of a sudden, you think, *was this how it was? Was this how it happened?* A moment so boring, you're already thinking of the next boring moment, and the one after that. *Is this it?* Lifting and tapping a cantaloupe, looking for black, welting spots on an heirloom tomato, thinking of the week's lunch or lesson you haven't yet planned. Picturing your students on Monday morning, staring into the white board's clean, blank face. Waiting. Remembering all those times you hushed their panic during lockdown drills, as you shoved your heads underneath tables and desks. You thought yourself ready. *Is it? This?* Funny how life happens, no, funny how life needs death for it to happen, be compared to. Valued. But you knew this already. Coming in from the parking lot, barely missing that red light. You knew. Just as elsewhere, someone is slipping their feet into a new pair of shoes, while parents set the table for breakfast, sisters get ready to sell raffle tickets, And brothers forget to heave their hearts to their throats before getting into their cars, rushing for a carton of milk they meant to buy earlier that week. They knew, too. You hope. Every one of them.

PORTRAIT OF AN ABSENT BROTHER

The way his fingers
pushed back
my hair—
this is what I choose to remember.

MORDIDA

God came down the valley one dust-covered day.
Told you to gather His flock. He spoke slowly
and carried a passport. Rounded his shoulders to get closer
to you. His speech was low and raspy like a headmaster's
or the hot wind that capsizes rowboats on summer nights.
The one that makes widows out of wives. He was looking
for two just men who had fallen off the wagon again.
Asked you to roll up your sleeves. Asked if you had ever shot a gun.
If your conscience was clean. Asked if you spoke English.
If you paid off your loans. Asked for your credit score.
¿Caballero, cómo nos arreglamos? To enter into this kingdom,
he said, you must pay the toll. He folded up your documents
and smacked the palm of His hand with them, waiting impatiently
for your response. Where is your brother, He asked?
What is the circumference of your wound?
What can you do with your mouth? Let's see it.
Show me what's under your tongue.
Do you own anything that isn't your shadow?
Why are you shaking? He scooped you up like a yearling.
His hands were soft but firm.
He could break you like morning bread.
What can you tell me about the rooms you've ruined?
I'm going to touch you now.
Are there any areas that are tender, sensitive?
What else besides your body do you carry
that is illegal? Will your body also carry bullets one day?
What other type of dark alphabet do you know?
Write it down. You keep shaking.

I'm only going to ask you this one more time.
How is it you keep going
when so many who look like you are dead?
Keep dying. Tell me, how many more elegies
do you still have left inside you?

WHAT'S ABOVE US IS EITHER DEAD OR STILL DYING

Suddenly, there's the urge to ruin
every garden I see,
uproot every goddamn flower
until my hands are the throbbing red

that traumatizes most people.
It's no longer hunting season, which means
I can roam freely with the others
if they'll have me. They won't.

To live through the breakdown,
one must first understand
the thing that breaks
is constantly breaking, quietly.

As such, I tried to go unnoticed,
swept all the rooms I'd been in
before exiting. Leaving behind
a certain kind of warmth in cushions

and furniture, unique to those types
of animals that know of no master's
touch. And I think of myself lucky
having survived all these years

calming my own blood down
whenever it felt loud and unbearable,
and I was alone. Have been alone
and will be. By this time of night,

the foragers have crept back
to their rooms, sleeping off
the afternoon's chores, leaning
into their loved ones, leaning into

their very own flesh, the art
they get to live in. Clean and unadorned.
It is quiet enough for me to see myself
as something other than tragic.

More than an itch on the palm's
open surface. As vast and with purpose
as the sky above, silently spreading itself
over my little, borrowed room.

ANGELO IS PROBABLY DEAD,
THE OFFICER TOLD MY MOTHER

Until then, I'd never seen strangers pray
like that, the way they did on that day.

When at the police station,
the officer told us you

were probably in a ditch or an empty lot
somewhere. Dead. Body twisted

in a final pose. I imagined you:
face turned away, deep in the dirt.

You were still beautiful. Elegant.
A child of light. And after those cold,

callous words were hurled at us
like gunshots, the women joined us.

Prayed the way only mothers pray.
Honest. Forgiving. Almost mean.

Down on their knees as if looking
for you in the ground. Angelo,

I am angry. I have no more
grievances in me. The world wants us

to be a damaged cathedral.
Wants us to be saved so badly.

Split us open with the Holy Ghost. We prayed.
In the officer's mind, you were somewhere

in a foreign town. Lifeless, already split
wide open like a dead dog's jaw.

A PROTAGONIST ONCE SAID

You took away the humming
   from my lungs.
Those quivering songs about misery
   and mourning doves,
with feathered chests bleeding,
    gone. In the only dreams
I remember, you are in a courtyard,
   a meadow slowly disappearing.
Please don't let me disappear.
   When I said I wanted you to leave,
I meant I didn't want you to stay, starving.
   I didn't know that then,
living in cities with sharp edges
   and antidepressants
   puncturing me.
How much I wanted to stay too.
   The letters you left are still sealed
in their envelopes. A fantastic logic rattling
   inside a yellowing smock. I didn't know you
could slip away too. Somewhere there's a boat
   floating on ancient waters.
      Gentle but dark.
What are bridges for if not to cross or burn them?
   Where you've gone, do you
get to see your father? When I'm gone,
    who will mourn us?
I step down from your sonnet, open the iron gate,
    and lean into your wonder.
You cup my face with your hands, and I laugh
   as if there is no tomorrow,
for some of us, there isn't.

LETTERS FROM A YOUNGER BROTHER, MOURNING

DAY TWELVE

Brother, you've been reduced to crumbs,
left on the side of the road for the sparrows to fight over.
I'm still here finding excuses not to make myself
thinner again, not counting the folds on my stomach
in front of the mirror so I could be adored the way a pop star
will be adored after leaving this tired realm of prescriptions
and overdoses. They say you are the missing shape
we've built ourselves around. We should be happy
with the memories we've hoarded. I'm not.

DAY TWENTY

Nothing prepares you to dream about bullets,
but you can still discern their sound even in your sleep.
The same sound you discerned since you were six,

when the neighborhood boys showed you
how to hide behind a parked car or pony wall,
making your body into the smallest shape

imaginable. How to outrun what seems unavoidable.
their noise fracturing the air like the wailing cry
of a siren or a celebratory firecracker. You remember.

How others fell to that music as if in a trance.
Figures contracting then collapsing into the night.
A light coating of stardust decorating the ground.

DAY THIRTY-FIVE

Once, for a man, I opened my mouth so wide
he swore he could see my grief. Made him lick it up
like a puddle of his own mess. I was fucked up.
Can't even blame it on lust, but loss, like hunger, will bring
anything to its knees. Doesn't matter what he believed.
He took what he could get. Every last drop of me,
I gave up. Long ago. When I bent over
the toilet and stared myself down, my pathetic reflection
was the only one waiting to release the fist
that was lodged in the back of my throat.

Look. I'm no saint. I gagged like the rest of them,
learned submission from you. Starved to avoid
the salty taste of a good-looking man. Starved
after having a taste of that man.
I want you to understand: maybe
I wanted to be devoured, taken in
by some dark impulse I could claim as my own.
The morsels of grief you left behind
make up the parts I can't reach, even to scratch.
They back me into a corner, plucking away
at my voice, ripping it apart like a useless receipt.

DAY SIXTY-SEVEN

Even the trees are sad.

DAY TWO-THIRTEEN

There is no *sincerely*, no *regards*.
You've moved through me like a traveling wound,
one day here, the next day—elsewhere.
I want to feel you leave my body

the way faith left my body many years ago.
Since then, everything insists on rhyming
with grief. From one language to the next,
grieving stays the same, no envelope can contain it.

Soon I'll lose count of the days. Forget.
I don't know if I'll do it intentionally or not.

DAY * * * *

You know how the story goes: When Cain killed
Abel, his blood sang to the Lord who asked:
Where is your brother? What have you done?

How do we outrun the unavoidable?
Sometimes, you must return to the source
of your greatest hurt. The first heartbreak,

your lowest test score. The impacted tooth
at the end of your memory's mouth. A gun
against a temple. How bad does it hurt?

You hear the tragedy before you can see it,
feel it. God knew all along about the lie:
Cain's sin. And you know how the world ends
not with noise or sobbing but with song.

RECUPERADO

In a dream, my brother returns.
 Fingers intact, ears untouched,
tongue at rest behind
 a row of unharmed teeth: a hammer
learning its own language.
 We are relieved, devoured by joy.
My mother tumbles upward
 from the ground where she's been
grieving. She stretches her hand
 to stroke the face we thought was lost
long ago. Her breath sticks to him
 like a soft clump of moss and everything
is slower than usual,
 and I begin now to think
maybe there is a God
 listening from his impossible seat
to the stinging prayers pouring out
 of this discarded one's lips, allowing
this moment, however small,
 to exist, to walk through the wavering
walls of disbelief and press
 my ear to the dealer's chest
right before the day, with its greed
 and labor, tears us apart. A God
to make of me that prophet coming back
 to his glittering source, to that hunger
that will possess him to speak
 first of beauty and then humiliation.

PORTRAIT OF THE SPEAKER
INSIDE A BURNING HOUSE

When I wanted to speak, I couldn't. There was an Inca dove roosting
in my lungs. My teeth were sharp as bullets. Deadly too.
I wrung my hands together. I ached. They said violence was the only song

I understood. Those mean lyrics struck me down unexpectedly,
one afternoon, while trying to get the firstborn to sleep.
They said all good stories begin with light, even the tragedies.

So here I am, gradually finding my way out of darkness.
Coywolves yelp outside my window, announcing their triumph
over a thing smaller than their skulls. They aren't the only ones

baring their appetite. I want to go back. Be less sweet. Feral.
How many matchbooks will it take? I want summer. Permanently.
A season of arrogance and heat. Several fevers hang on the clothesline.

The back of my neck, smeared and shiny as though I am a thing of value.
I press my face against the open flame. A paper wasp gets stranded inside,
fluttering and buzzing itself into exhaustion. Near death. Against

the wooden panels. I gently scoop it into a cup before releasing it
through the screen door. For a while, I was cold until I wasn't.

BROOMTAIL BALLAD

June: the ants do what ants do to a wounded thing.
They hunger. I do too. You'll find me unabashedly biting

the heads off flowers. Grinding the petals between
my crooked teeth. I've grown tired of metaphors.

Of being pleasant. I've tried hard to forget about the boy
shot down near the empty parking lot. The girls who keep

vanishing in the desert, near dusk. Some found hog-tied,
some not found at all. Each one still a prayer inside

a mother's mouth. A bead in a necklace they hold with their fists.
Somedays, I forget the last names of the ones I've loved.

Rub my hands together to conjure up heat, to remember.
I've stayed up all night, pushing away my darkness.

Outside, there's a buck who walks around the cathedral grounds.
Looking for lost fawns. Sometimes, I almost believe it's you.

Reminding me of my good fortune. Telling me to stay
untamed. Hell-bent. Soon, I'll take the body of a man,

a stranger, a good brother, on my tongue. Lord, deliver me
from harm. Rid the fear in my throat. I want to believe.

Wholeheartedly. I do. Without shame. Believe. One day.
You'll remove the smell of gunpowder from my skin.

THE SIMPLE HOUR

You left to be with the horses,
high-necked but bruised as midnight.

I counted every muscle on you, at least
when dreaming. In youth, you were mistaken

for a mule, body lurching away
from excellence. You could have been

the herd's head, the strongest bite
to bare the fields. I wanted more

for you. Come shape my stupidity again
as if there were feed enough

to keep you. Be like the moon,
serving her peasants the palest gold.

COWBOY PARK

This is my home/this thin edge/of barbed wire

—GLORIA ANZALDÚA

*

I want to rename all of the constellations after you, but I know the sky was not meant for us, made like the other things we made out of construction paper from our childhood imagination—black creased canvas, skewed and punctured with the sharp end of a screw. Taped to a lopsided cardboard backdrop, spray-painted silver. Our diorama always ended in disappointment. This was all we knew.

* *

The fatherless neighborhood, the cracked asphalt hurting our feet, a pickup truck rusting in the driveway: accurate depictions of our future traumas. And here we found the valuables: the shiny shell casings, bottle caps, and syringes. Poor man's jewelry. The games of asking ourselves which of these gleams the loudest. We were two brown boys mistaken for brothers. Too young to be that wise and broken.

* * *

On our knees, near the playground where some teens overdosed a few summers ago, we nicknamed ourselves after what could harm us. While divvying up this inheritance, we conspired to be beautiful and vowed to live even in the dullest light. Remember? How harmless it seemed to be Boy-Gods digging through the dirt, making our own turf, our own beasts and rules. Carving away our own stars, cutting open the wild animal belly of the heavens, letting it bleed out slowly.

* * * *

Now, there's only one of us. I have made words my occupation, while you lie somewhere silently under the earth. Face fixed upward, arms pressed to your sides like an instrument stored away for safekeeping. The trees stoop closer, leaning in like men offering up a secret or their condolences. And

85

even with your eyes closed and long gone, you can't deny that I counted my blessings, my lucky stars—all in order. I took inventory of my wounds; became an injured room. No one dares to visit.

* * * * *

Even after all these distances, I'm still attracted to what's damaged: a bird with a missing wing, a man who asked me to slap him during sex. He liked the same hurt he felt from his father. Another one who said he had a snake in his brain. He was a hard worker. Impassioned and naive. Reformed. I grew sick of his pleasantries, so he gifted me his wish list of obscenities. *This isn't my first rodeo*, I told him. I say this to remind myself of how fortunate I turned out. How brutal.

* * * * * *

From the foot of the bed, I still call to you, waiting for a response loud enough to reach me. *From where you rest, what do the stars look like?*

Tell me: *What do we look like to the heavens?*

MUSTANG

If there's a carousel somewhere—*anywhere*—you better believe
I'm riding it. Even at the end of the world. The unforgivable ones
can vouch for me. They'll tell you about the feral-boy-turned-man,

refusing to get down. Eyes closed, head tilted back, mouth wide open,
one hand tightly gripping the stiff mane and the other one fixed over
the glossy bridle on the horse's grinning, cartoon face. Let them know

about my unfettered joy: those dark-haired beauties. Whinnying.
Always in motion. Gears slowly squeaking with rhythm.
Never struggling to stop. Don't pray for me anymore.

If I don't come back, rejoice. It will be the only love I'll have.
Before the rivers dry up and all the pastures get picked clean.
I'll no longer embrace a master's name or call. The snap

of cruel fingers. The badlands. I'll understand why the ground
rattles with the weight of its own murmuring. I'll appreciate
the dust's hymn. The wind's back and forth motion. Spinning me away.

I won't comb my hair. I won't come back. Picture me like this:
marvelous and wild. Bucking under the light. The heat of bulbs,
warming my brown skin. My brown joy. Galloping in the ever after.

PURGATORY

for my traumas

I place them on the dance floor:
Those muscled-marbled sweet talkers

and go-go boys in neon-colored jockstraps,
bulges bursting with wads of bills and something extra.

The ones named after emperors and spiders.
Blowing off their week's pay on poppers

and spiked seltzers. No one loves them
the way I do. Knowing they are always there—

down the spiraling steps of my memory—
gives me comfort. I visit them occasionally.

To feel the heat I once craved. The one
cradling me back to my bed,

when all I can think about is grief
and climbing out of things that no longer

serve me. On those Friday nights when piles
of papers are stacked on the nightstand, waiting

to be marked, I imagine their hands ushering me
through the door, the bouncer stamping

my wrist before I enter, joining them at the center
of their inner circle. Pushed back and forth

against their chests and biceps. Swaying.
They lick my neck and clavicles clean, offer

to French-kiss the filth out of me, leave their scent
behind. And for a while, I don't feel shame,

or that suffering that was let loose on my life
like a tick-bitten mutt once chained

to a fence in the backyard long ago.
I don't blame them. Instead, I stay

a bit longer, relieved I can always
come back. Relishing, for once, their bite,

their light. Feeling their godlike generosity,
lessons, and morals. Feeling for once

their electric nerves and currents, their presence
running through me. An endless trope.

A rope. Unshakeable. To them, I dedicate a park, a street,
parts of a childhood river that felt uneasy.

Ferocious at first. I meant to tell them I won't return
but they know, as I do, that is untrue.

I'll stay for the after-party and long after that.
Smoke something that will burn my lungs on a terrace,

overlooking the underworld, a hand gently stroking
my head, another one unbuttoning me out of my pants.

The life above this one slides its feet across the floor.
Shifts its weight. I can feel it. Just as I can still feel

the stinging mark of a slap on my cheek as I leave
the door ajar when I'm ready to go home. Staggering

upward to the forgiving force. The brilliant one,
who's slowly stirring coffee in a cup, bringing a spoon

closer to their lips. The one who's been up all night,
deeply worried, waiting to tell me how much they've missed me.

PORTRAIT OF THE SPEAKER
RIDING A GREYHOUND BUS

After putting away all of the cowboys, you take yourself to the farthest
part of the country: the cold, closed hand of America. You aren't hopeful
but pray in secret, leaving behind apartments with pets that aren't yours

but are family. You've been alone for so long. Forget
those well-known disasters: the motion sickness, the bill collectors,
those big rigs jackknifed on the road, your preoccupation

with shipwrecks. They were never useful to you. The scent
from your past life, sealed in care packages gifted to you,
rebuke it. You'll sleep well. Make sure of it. From your window seat,

the autumn light of this coastal town pours in. Trust it.
Open yourself to those houses shaped like fishhooks,
the secondhand stores whose doors swelled from last night's rain.

The souvenir shops where men use sharp tools to whittle wood
for keepsakes. The dive bars with leather harnesses hanging
from awnings, swinging in the wind like pig carcasses hoisted up

to greet you. Perhaps you'll find yourself stumbling back
to your room in the early hours, shirt untucked, mind a dizzied mess
of delights. Let it all in. From head to toe and all the way back up again.

Today, you'll see a sailboat making its way to what seems
like the earth's edge. Your eyes will focus on it as if it were
the most beautiful sentence you've ever read. Unedited or revised.

Dusk will close in soon, and you'll follow that tiny boat over the glimmering waves. Letting the full context of it travel through you. You'll follow it until it disappears, you'll follow it until you realize you've witnessed God for the first time.

Notes

The opening epigraph is from the essay "How to Tame a Wild Tongue" in the book *Borderlands/La Frontera: The New Mestiza* by Gloria Anzaldúa.

The second epigraph is from "the border is . . . (a manifesto)" from the book *Warrior for Gringostroika* by Guillermo Gómez Peña.

The poem "Portrait of My Mother Studying for Her Citizenship Exam" references Patrick Henry's famous line, "Give me liberty or give me death," from his speech during the Second Virginia Convention of 1775, and contains the phrase "Pobre México, tan lejos de Dios y tan cerca de Estados Unidos," which was coined by the journalist Nemesio García Naranjo and popularized by the thirty-third president of México, Porfirio Díaz.

The poem "Vaquero" adapts a line from the song "Every Rose Has Its Thorn" by the band Poison. The line, "No one gets between me and my vaqueros," references Brooke Shields's 1980s ad for Calvin Klein.

The poem "Negation Litany for a Fallen God" includes a lyric from 2 Live Crew's "Face Down, Ass Up."

The epigraph in the poem "Cowboy Park," "This is my home/this thin edge/of barbed wire," is from the essay "The Homeland, Aztlán, El Otro México" from Gloria Anzaldúa's *Borderlands/La Frontera: The New Mestiza*.

Acknowledgments

Para mi familia, aquí y en el más allá: Rebeca Perez Castro, Gilberto Perez, Gloria Leyva, the Martínez crew: Saul, Hugo, Ulises, Joel, Jonathan, Sebastian, Ixchel, Marcos e Israel. Mil gracias por todo su apoyo y por enseñarme como ser ingenioso, trabajador, fuerte, y seguro de mi mismo. Su presencia e historias me ayudaron a cultivar mis talentos y mi creatividad. Gracias por permitirme soñar y por dejarme seguir soñando. ¡Para ustedes todos mis respetos!

To my chosen family, professors, and mentors who nurtured this work, recognizing the words and literature that simmered in me, and who breathed new life into it: Rosa Alcalá, Benjamin Alire Saenz, Eduardo C. Corral, Dr. Ernesto Chavez, Timothy Donnelly, C. Dale Young, Maudelle Driskell, Liz Johnson, Ben Garcia, Rigoberto González, Juan Luis Guzman, Sarug Sarano, Emmy Perez, Lex Williford, Alan Gilbert, Mark Wunderlich, Tracy K. Smith, Lynn Melnick, Phillip B. Williams, Evie Shockley, Noy Holland, Vicki Vargas, Zeynep Özakat, Laura Cresté, Mark Bibbins, Cate Marvin, Alice Quinn, Hannah Webster, Samyak Shertok, Tracy Fuad, Shastri Akella, Sterling HolyWhiteMountain, Molly Anders, Anthony Cody, Mai Der Vang, Vanessa Angélica Villarreal, Natalie Scenters-Zapico, Rosebud Ben-Oni, Brent Ameneyro, Ashley Gonzalez, Francisco y Mercedes Araiza, Shanique Pinnock, Katy Saintil, Scott Shanahan, Donna Denizé, Yi-Na Chung, Corey and Cameron Klein, and King, the cat. Thank you for always believing in me and supporting me throughout this process. With your guidance and light, this work was possible.

A huge shout-out to the Lambda Literary poetry cohort under the tutelage of Philip B. Williams.

To my fellow educators and students for your constant encouragement.

To my luminous one, Lucie Brock-Broido, for your love, support, light, and countless blessings. My kingdom has arrived.

Y por supuesto, thank you to Troy Montes-Michie for inspiring me to go through the door with my words and ideas. You are remarkable. Te quiero, güey. My one and only. Eres la mera, mera patineta. Para ti, todo mi corazón!

I am deeply grateful to the editors of the following journals who first published versions of these poems: *Apogee Journal, The Journal, The Cincinnati Review, The Hopkins Review, The Boston Review, Best New Poets 2015, Nepantla: A Journal Dedicated to Queer Poets of Color, Nimrod International Journal, Frontier Poetry, Bettering American Poetry,* the *Los Angeles Review, Assaracus Journal, EPOCH Magazine, The Account, Foglifter,* and *Poetry Magazine.*

Thanks to the following organizations and residencies for granting me the time and space to grow as a writer: CantoMundo, The Frost Place, the Fine Arts Work Center in Provincetown, Lambda Literary, The Juniper Summer Writing Institute, Poets & Writers, and St. Alban's School.

Lastly, I am grateful to Amaud Jamaul Johnson and the Wisconsin Poetry Series. Thanks to Sean Bishop, Jackie Krass, Dennis Lloyd, Allie Shay, and the fantastic team at the University of Wisconsin Press who made this dream come true. ¡Mil Gracias!

WISCONSIN POETRY SERIES

Sean Bishop and Jesse Lee Kercheval, series editors
Ronald Wallace, founding series editor

How the End First Showed (B) • D. M. Aderibigbe

New Jersey (B) • Betsy Andrews

Salt (B) • Renée Ashley

(At) Wrist (B) • Tacey M. Atsitty

Horizon Note (B) • Robin Behn

What Sex Is Death? (T) • Dario Bellezza, selected and translated by
  Peter Covino

About Crows (FP) • Craig Blais

Mrs. Dumpty (FP) • Chana Bloch

Shopping, or The End of Time (FP) • Emily Bludworth de Barrios

The Declarable Future (4L) • Jennifer Boyden

The Mouths of Grazing Things (B) • Jennifer Boyden

Help Is on the Way (4L) • John Brehm

No Day at the Beach • John Brehm

Sea of Faith (B) • John Brehm

Reunion (FP) • Fleda Brown

Brief Landing on the Earth's Surface (B) • Juanita Brunk

Ejo: Poems, Rwanda, 1991–1994 (FP) • Derick Burleson

Grace Engine • Joshua Burton

The Roof of the Whale Poems (T) • Juan Calzadilla, translated by
  Katherine M. Hedeen and Olivia Lott

Jagged with Love (B) • Susanna Childress

Almost Nothing to Be Scared Of (4L) • David Clewell

The Low End of Higher Things • David Clewell

(B) = Winner of the Brittingham Prize in Poetry
(FP) = Winner of the Felix Pollak Prize in Poetry
(4L) = Winner of the Four Lakes Prize in Poetry
(T) = Winner of the Wisconsin Prize for Poetry in Translation

Don't Explain (FP) • Betsy Sholl

House of Sparrows: New and Selected Poems (4L) • Betsy Sholl

Late Psalm • Betsy Sholl

Otherwise Unseeable (4L) • Betsy Sholl

Blood Work (FP) • Matthew Siegel

Fruit (4L) • Bruce Snider

The Year We Studied Women (FP) • Bruce Snider

Bird Skin Coat (B) • Angela Sorby

The Sleeve Waves (FP) • Angela Sorby

If the House (B) • Molly Spencer

Wait (B) • Alison Stine

Hive (B) • Christina Stoddard

The Red Virgin: A Poem of Simone Weil (B) • Stephanie Strickland

The Room Where I Was Born (B) • Brian Teare

Fragments in Us: Recent and Earlier Poems (FP) • Dennis Trudell

Girl's Guide to Leaving • Laura Villareal

The Apollonia Poems (4L) • Judith Vollmer

Level Green (B) • Judith Vollmer

Reactor • Judith Vollmer

The Sound Boat: New and Selected Poems (4L) • Judith Vollmer

Voodoo Inverso (FP) • Mark Wagenaar

Hot Popsicles • Charles Harper Webb

Liver (FP) • Charles Harper Webb

The Blue Hour (B) • Jennifer Whitaker

American Sex Tape (B) • Jameka Williams

Centaur (B) • Greg Wrenn

Pocket Sundial (B) • Lisa Zeidner